WEAVING IT TOGETHER

1

Milada Broukal

Glendale Community College

Heinle & Heinle Publishers
A Division of Wadsworth, Inc.
Boston, Massachusetts 02116 U.S.A.

The publication of *Weaving It Together 1* was directed by members of the Newbury House Publishing Team at Heinle & Heinle:

Erik Gundersen, **Editorial Director**
Kristin Thalheimer, **Production Editor**

Also participating in the publication of this program were:

Publisher: Stanley J. Galek
Editorial Production Manager: Elizabeth Holthaus
Associate Editor: Karen Hazar
Associate Marketing Manager: Donna Hamilton
Project Manager: Hockett Editorial Service
Manufacturing Coordinator: Mary Beth Lynch
Photo Coordinator: Martha Leibs-Heckly
Production Assistant: Maryellen Eschmann
Interior Designer: Winston • Ford Visual Communications
Illustrator: James Edwards
Cover Illustrator: Lisa Houck
Cover Designer: Judy Ziegler

Photo Credits (page numbers are given in boldface):
1—Ulrike Welsch **3**—Elizabeth Crews, Stock, Boston **11**—Stock, Boston **23**—Georg Gerster, Comstock (China); Peter Menzel, Stock, Boston, (Mexico); SuperStock (Hollywood) **24**—SuperStock **47**—Gale Zucker, Stock, Boston **48**—Ulrike Welsch **57**—SuperStock **67**—Katrina Thomas, Photo Researchers, Inc. **68**—FourbyFive **77**—Janet M. Milhomme **87**—Scala/Art Resource/Arcimboldo: L'Ortolano **88**—Catherine Ursillo, Photo Researchers, Inc. **105**—Volker Kramer-Stern, Voller Ernst/Komische Fotos **106**—Comstock **116**—John C. Lei Studios Inc., Stock, Boston **127**—Cary Wolinsky, Stock, Boston (MLK Jr); Milton Feinberg, Stock, Boston (Ozawa); SuperStock (Indira Gandhi) **128**—UPI/Bettmann **138**—Phyllis Graber Jensen, Stock, Boston

· ·

Heinle & Heinle Publishers is a division of Wadsworth, Inc.

Manufactured in the United States of America

Library of Congress Cataloging-in-Publication Data
Broukal, Milada.
      Weaving it together.

      1. English language—Textbooks for foreign speakers.
I. Title.
PE1128.B715   1993   428.2′4   92-43932
ISBN 0-8384-4221-8 (v. 1)
ISBN 0-8384-3977-2 (v. 2)
ISBN 0-8384-4222-6 (v. 3)

CONTENTS

Unit 3: Health

Unit 4: Customs

Unit 5: Food

Unit 6: Inventions

TO THE TEACHER

Rationale

Weaving It Together, Book 1, is the first in a three-book series that integrates reading and writing skills for students of English as a second or foreign language. The complete program includes the following:

Book 1 . . . Beginning level

Book 2 . . . High beginning level

Book 3 . . . Intermediate level

The central premise of *Weaving It Together* is that reading and writing are interwoven and inextricable skills. Good readers write well; good writers read well. With this premise in mind, *Weaving It Together* has been developed to meet the following objectives:

1. To combine reading and writing through a comprehensive, systematic, and engaging process designed to effectively integrate the two.
2. To provide academically bound students with serious and engaging multicultural content.
3. To promote individualized and cooperative learning within the moderate to large-sized class.

Over the past few years, a number of noted researchers in the field of second-language acquisition have written about the serious need to effectively integrate reading and writing instruction in both classroom practice and materials development. *Weaving It Together* is, in many ways, a response to this need.

Barbara Kroll, for example, talks of teaching students to read like writers and write like readers (1993). She notes: "It is only when a writer is able to cast himself or herself in the role of a reader of the text under preparation that he or she is able to anticipate the reader's needs by writing into the text what he or she expects or wants the reader to take out from the text." Through its systematic approach to integrating reading and writing, *Weaving It Together* teaches ESL and EFL students to understand the kinds of interconnections between reading and writing which they need to make in order to achieve academic success.

Linda Lonon Blanton's research focuses on the need for second-language students to develop authority, conviction, and certainty in their writing. She believes that students develop strong writing skills in concert with good reading skills. Blanton writes: "My experience tells me that empowerment, or achieving this certainty and authority, can be achieved only through performance—through the act of speaking and writing about texts, through developing individual responses to texts." (1992)

For Blanton, as for Kroll and others, both reading and writing must be treated as composing processes. Effective writing instruction must be integrally linked with effective reading instruction. This notion is at the heart of *Weaving It Together*.

Organization of the Text

Weaving It Together, Book 1, contains seven thematically organized units, each of which includes two interrelated chapters. Each chapter begins with a reading, moves on to a set of activities designed to develop critical reading skills, and culminates with a series of interactive writing exercises.

Each chapter contains the following sequence of activities:

1. **Pre-reading questions:** Each chapter is introduced with a page of photographs or drawings accompanied by a set of discussion questions. The purpose of the pre-reading questions is to prepare students for the reading by activating their background knowledge and encouraging them to call on and share their experiences.

2. **Reading:** Each reading is a high-interest, nonfiction passage related to the theme of the unit. Selected topics include Sleep, A Baby's First Haircut, and Chocolate.

3. **Vocabulary:** The vocabulary in bold type in each reading passage is practiced in the vocabulary exercise which follows the passage. The vocabulary items introduced and practiced provide a useful source for students when they are writing their own sentences on the same theme.

4. **Comprehension:** There are two types of comprehension exercises: The first, *Looking for Main Ideas*, concentrates on a general understanding of the reading. This exercise may be done after a first silent reading of the text. Students can reread the text to check answers. The second comprehension exercise, *Looking for Details*, concentrates on developing skimming and scanning skills.

5. **Discussion:** Students may work in small or large groups and interact with one another to discuss questions that arise from the reading. These questions ask students to relate their experiences to what they have learned from the reading.

6. **Organizing:** With each of the fourteen readings a different aspect of writing at the sentence level is presented. These aspects include sentence word order, capitalization and punctuation, and the use of adjectives, adverbs, and prepositions. Exercises following the points taught are provided for reinforcement.

7. **Writing at the sentence level:** Using the ideas they have generated in the discussion section and the grammar points practiced, students write sentences about themselves in answer to the questions discussed in the lesson.

8. **Rewriting using the checklist:** Students rewrite sentences generated from the questions in the form of a paragraph. They use the checklist on their own or with a partner to check their paragraphs and make any necessary alterations. Teachers are encouraged to add any further points they consider important to the checklist provided.

9. **Editing your work:** In this section, students are encouraged to work with a partner or their teacher to correct spelling, punctuation, vocabulary, and grammar.

10. **Writing your final copy:** Students prepare the final version of the paragraph.

Journal Writing

In addition to the projects and exercises in the book, I strongly recommend that students be instructed to keep a journal in which they correspond with you. The purpose of this journal is for them to tell you how they feel about the class each day. It gives them an opportunity to tell you what they like, what they dislike, what they understand, and what they don't understand. By having students explain what they have learned in the class, you can discover whether or not they understand the concepts taught.

Journal writing is effective for two major reasons. First, since this type of writing focuses on fluency and personal expression, students always have something to write about. Second, journal writing can also be used to identify language concerns and troublespots which need further review. In its finest form, journal writing can become an active dialogue between teacher and student that permits you both to learn more about your students' lives and to individualize their language instruction.

References

Blanton, Linda Lonon (1992). "Reading, Writing, and Authority: Issues in Developmental ESL." *College ESL*, 2, 11–19.

Kroll, Barbara (1993). "Teaching Writing *Is* Teaching Reading: Training the New Teacher of ESL Composition" in *Reading in the Composition Classroom* (Heinle & Heinle Publishers, Boston), 61–81.

TO THE STUDENT

This book will teach you to read and write in English. You will study readings on selected themes and learn strategies for writing good sentences on those themes. In the process, you will learn to express your own ideas in sentences and work toward writing a paragraph in good English.

It is important for you to know that writing well in English may be quite different from writing well in your native language. Good Chinese or Arabic writing is different from good English writing. Not only are the styles different but the organization is different too. Good Spanish organization is different from good English organization.

The processes of reading and writing are closely interconnected. Therefore, in this text we are weaving reading and writing together. I hope that the readings in this text will stimulate your interest to write, and that *Weaving It Together* will make writing in English much easier for you.

Milada Broukal

ACKNOWLEDGMENTS

I would like to express my gratitude to the following individuals who reviewed *Weaving It Together, Book 1,* and who offered many ideas and suggestions: Cheryl Benz, Miami-Dade Community College; Barbara Rigby-Acosta, El Paso Community College; and Greg Conner, Orange Coast College.

My very special thanks to my wonderful editor Erik Gundersen for his insights and encouragement throughout this work. I am also grateful to Karen Hazar and the rest of the Heinle & Heinle team who worked on this project.

I would like to take this opportunity to thank my mother and father for their unremitting love and support throughout my projects.

UNIT 1

Special Days

Chapter 1: Birthdays

PRE-READING QUESTIONS

Discuss these questions with your classmates or teacher.

1 What do you see in the picture?

2 How is the birthday in the picture different from a birthday in your country?

3 Do you like birthdays? Why or why not?

Reading: Birthdays

Many children have a birthday cake with **candles** on their birthday. In some countries, like England and Scotland, there is another **custom**, too. There people **spank** or hit the child on his/her birthday. This may hurt a little, but they say it is very lucky for the child. The child must never cry. The custom says that if you cry, you will cry all year.

The reason for birthday spanks is to make the bad **spirits** go away. The harder you spank the better it is. In Belgium, another country in Europe, the custom is a little different. There a parent goes into the child's bedroom early in the morning with a **needle**. As soon as the child wakes up, the parent **pricks** the child with the needle. This is for good luck!

As you grow older, you get more spanks. You usually get one for each year plus an extra one.

Complete the sentences. Circle the letter of the correct answer.

1. A birthday cake has _____ on it.
   a. needles
   b. candles

2. England and Scotland have another _____.
   a. custom
   b. country

3. People in England and Scotland _____ the child on his/her birthday.
   a. wake
   b. spank

4. The reason for birthday spanks is to make the bad _____ go away.
   a. parents
   b. spirits

5. In Belgium, a parent goes into the child's bedroom with a _____.
   a. needle
   b. birthday

6. The parent _____ the child with a needle.
   a. pricks
   b. cries

A. Looking for the Main Ideas

Read the passage again and look for the MAIN IDEAS. Circle the letter of the correct answer.

1. On a child's birthday in England and Scotland, _____.

   a. people spank the child

   b. the child aways cries

   c. the child is not lucky

2. The reason for birthday spanks is _____.

   a. to make the spirits come

   b. to be different

   c. to make the bad spirits go away

3. On a child's birthday in Belgium, a parent _____.

   a. spanks the child

   b. pricks the child

   c. sleeps in the child's bedroom

B. Looking for Details

Read the passage again and look for DETAILS. Circle T if the sentence is true. Circle F if the sentence is false.

1. A birthday spank is very lucky for the parent.	T	F
2. Belgium is a country in England.	T	F
3. In Belgium the custom is a little different.	T	F
4. In Belgium a parent goes into the child's bedroom.	T	F
5. The parent pricks the child with a needle.	T	F
6. You get one spank for each year.	T	F

DISCUSSION

Discuss the answers to these questions with your classmates.

1. How do you usually celebrate a birthday in your country?

2. Are birthdays important in your country? Is another day, such as your name day or New Year's Day, more important?

3. Is it important to celebrate your birthday every year or only special years?

The Sentence

A sentence always has a subject and a verb. Many sentences also have an object. The sentence order in English is usually as follows:

Example:	subject	verb	object
	John	has	a birthday.
	(Subj.)	(Verb)	(Obj.)

The Subject

The *subject* is usually a noun, a pronoun, or a phrase with a noun. It tells us who is doing the action and usually comes before the verb.

Look at the subjects in the following sentences:
Examples:

> **John** has a birthday.
> (The subject is a noun.)
>
> **He** has a birthday.
> (The subject is a pronoun.)
>
> **The tall boy** has a birthday.
> (The subject is a phrase with a noun.)
>
> **The tall boy with black hair** has a birthday.
> (The prepositional phrase **with black hair** comes after the noun and is part of the whole subject.)

Exercise 1

Underline the subject in the sentences.

1. She has a brother.
2. Mary Peel loves children.
3. The tall woman has a birthday.
4. The tall woman with white hair has a birthday today.
5. Many children have a birthday cake.
6. Birthday spanks are a custom.
7. Customs in some countries are strange.
8. Parents in Belgium prick the child on his/her birthday.

The Verb

The verb tells us the action of the subject. Some verbs are one word, but some verbs are more than one word.

Example:

Mary <u>has</u> a birthday.
    (Verb)

Mary <u>is having</u> a birthday.
     (Verb)

Mary <u>is going to have</u> a birthday.
      (Verb)

Exercise 2

Underline the subject with one line and the verb with two lines in the following sentences.

1. He has many gifts.

2. The child cries.

3. The little girl is crying.

4. The little girl with the red hair is going to cry.

5. Many friends are going to say happy birthday.

Punctuation and Capitalization

A sentence always begins with a capital letter and ends with a period (.), an exclamation point (!), or a question mark (?). The first word after a comma (,) begins with a small letter.

Here are some rules for using capital letters.

Capitalization Rules

1. Capitalize the first word in a sentence.

   Many children have a birthday cake on their birthday.

2. Capitalize the pronoun **I**.

   John and I have the same birthday.

3. Capitalize all proper nouns. Here are some proper nouns:

a. Names of people and their titles:

Mr. John Sands	Ms. Mary Lee
Robert	Diana
Bob Briggs	Chan Lai Fong

b. Names of cities, states, and countries:

London, England   Houston, Texas
Acapulco   Hong Kong
Taiwan   Korea

c. Names of days and months:

Monday   Saturday
May   July
Friday   August

Exercise 3

Change the small letters to capital letters where necessary.

1. maria is from mexico city, mexico.
2. victor is from lima, peru.
3. ito and mayumi are from tokyo, japan.
4. the test is on monday, october 7.
5. mohammed's birthday is on tuesday, april 10.
6. wednesday, june 5th, is bob's birthday.
7. my sister suzie and i were born in february.
8. mrs. lee's birthday is in december.
9. mr. brown and i are going to a party on friday.
10. i am going to miami, florida, in july.

Write Sentences

Answer these questions with complete sentences. Use capital letters and periods where necessary.

1. What is your full name?

   _____

   _____

2. Where do you come from? (Give the city and country.)

   _____

   _____

3. When is your birthday?

   _____

   _____

4. Write the full name of another student in your class.

   _____

   _____

5. Where does he/she come from? (Give the city and country.)

   _____

   _____

6. When is his/her birthday?

   _____

   _____

7. What do you usually do on your birthday (have a birthday cake, a party, go out)?

   _____

   _____

8. What does your friend usually do on his/her birthday?

_____

_____

9. Will you remember your friend's birthday now? (You have the date on this page.)

_____

_____

Chapter 2: New Year's Day

PRE-READING QUESTIONS

Discuss these questions with your classmates or teacher.

1 What are the people doing in the picture?

2 When do you celebrate the New Year in your country?

3 Do you go out or stay at home for the New Year celebration?

Reading: New Year's Day

The Chinese New Year is the most important holiday for the Chinese people. For the Chinese, the New Year comes with the first day of the First Moon, between January 21 and February 19. People prepare for the holiday for fifteen days.

Finally, at midnight it is New Year's Day or the first day of the First Moon, Yuan Tan. People close the shops and the streets are **empty**. Everyone **locks** the doors and stays at home.

It is an important time for the family. The younger people **bow** to the older people. The Chinese call this K'ou T'ou or kowtow. This means "to touch the **ground** with the **forehead**." Then the younger people wish the older people a happy New Year. The older people give children gifts of money in red envelopes. The family then goes to sleep.

In the morning, everything is quiet. People dress in their best clothes. They are very **polite** and do not use bad words. People stay home. It is very quiet in the streets.

VOCABULARY

Complete the definitions. Circle the letter of the correct answer.

1. When there is nobody in a place, the place is _____.

    a. important

    b. empty

2. When you close the door and turn the key, you _____ the door.

    a. lock

    b. open

3. When you lower your head or put the top part of your body forward to show respect, you _____.

    a. touch

    b. bow

4. The part of the face above the eyes and below the hair is the _____.

    a. forehead

    b. ear

5. When you have good manners, you are _____.

    a. happy

    b. polite

6. In a house we use the word "floor"; for the same thing outside we use the word _____.

    a. home

    b. ground

A. Looking for the Main Ideas

Write complete answers to these questions.

1. What is the most important holiday for the Chinese people?

   _____

   _____

2. When is the Chinese New Year?

   _____

   _____

3. For whom is this an important time?

   _____

   _____

B. Looking for Details

One word in each sentence is not correct. Rewrite the sentence with the correct word.

1. The Chinese New Year comes with the first day of the First Year, between January 21 and February 19.

   _____

   _____

2. Chinese people prepare for the holiday for twenty-one days.

   _____

   _____

3. Everyone opens the doors and stays at home.

   _____

   _____

4. The older people give children gifts of clothes in red envelopes.

_____

_____

5. People dress in their quiet clothes.

_____

_____

6. They are very happy and do not use bad words.

_____

_____

DISCUSSION

Discuss these questions with your classmates.

1. What do people wear for the New Year in your country?
2. What kinds of food do they eat?
3. Do people give or get gifts on this day?
4. How is the American celebration of the New Year different from the celebration in your country? (as far as you know)

Sentence Order

As we know from **Chapter 1,** *sentence order in English is usually as follows:*

subject   **verb**   **object**

The **verb** does the action. The **subject** tells us who is doing the action. The **object** answers the question "what?"

The Object

The object *can be a noun, a pronoun, or a noun phrase. The action of the subject and verb produces the object.*

Examples:

Everyone locks the doors.
(S)   (V)   (Obj.)

Older people give gifts of money.
(S)   (V)   (Obj.)

The Complement

Some verbs are not action verbs; they are linking verbs. They are verbs like **be, become, seem,** *and* **feel.** *These verbs may be followed by a noun, noun phrase, or adjective. This is called a* **complement.**

Examples:

It is quiet.
(S) (V) (Comp.)

They are special dishes.
(S) (V)   (Comp.)

Exercise 1

Underline the objects or complements in these sentences.

1. People close the shops.
2. The streets are empty.
3. The older people give red envelopes.
4. The Chinese New Year is important.
5. Our family prepares special food.
6. People wear their best clothes.
7. Many people visit neighbors.
8. Relatives bring many gifts.

Punctuation and Capitalization

Remember that a sentence always begins with a capital letter and ends with a period (.), an exclamation point (!), or a question mark (?).

Here are some more rules for using capital letters.

Capitalization Rules

1. Capitalize names of nationalities, races, languages, and religions.

American	Chinese
Moslem	Catholic
Hispanic	Asian
Italian	Arab

2. Capitalize names of special days.

New Year's Day	Independence Day
Christmas	Halloween

Exercise 2

Change the small letters to capital letters where necessary.

1. we do not have classes during christmas and easter vacation.

2. on new year's day we stay at home.

3. the american woman celebrated chinese new year with us.

4. in our class we have students who are buddhist, moslem, christian, and jewish.

5. for us new year's day is more important than christmas.

6. all over the united states on july 4 americans celebrate independence day.

1. Write sentences.

Answer these questions with complete sentences. Use capital letters and periods where necessary.

a. What is the most important holiday in your country?

_____

_____

b. When do you celebrate it?

_____

_____

c. What do you wear on this holiday?

_____

_____

d. Where do you go?

_____

_____

e. What food do you prepare or eat?

_____

_____

f. Do you give/get gifts?

_____

_____

g. Why is this holiday important?

2. Rewrite in paragraph form.

Rewrite your sentences in the form of the paragraph below:

```
                                                    Name
                                                    Date
                                                    ESL 120
                          Title
........................................................................
      XXXXXXXXXXXXXXXXXXXXXXXXXXXXXXXXXXXXXXXXXXXXXX
   XXXXXXXXXXXXXXXXXXXXXXXXXXXXXXXXXXXXXXXXXXXXXXXXX
   XXXXXXXXXXXXXXXXXXXXXXXXXXXXXXXXXXXXXXXXXXXXXXXXX
   XXXXXXXXXXXXXXXXXXXXXXXXXXXXXXXXXXXXXXXXXXXXXXXXX
   XXXXXXXXXXXXXXXXXXXXXXXXXXXXXXXXXXXXXXXXXXXXXXXXX
   XXXXXXXXXXXXXXXXXXXXXXXXXXXXXXXXXXXXXXXXXXXXXXXXX
   XXXXXXXXXXXXXXXXXXXXXXXXXXXXXXXXXXXXXXXXXXXXXXXXX
   XXXXXXXXXXXXXXXXXXXXXXXXXXXXXXXXXXXXXXXXXXXXXXXXX
   XXXXXXXXXXXXXXXXXXXXXXXXXXXXXXXXXXXXXXXXXXXXXXXXX
   XXXXXXXXXXXXXXXXXXXXXXXXXXXXXXXXXXXXXXXXXXXXXXXXX
   XXXXXXXXXXXXXXXXXXXXXXXXXXXXXXXXXXXXXXXXXXXXXXXXX
```

Paragraph Form

It is important that you start to write using the form of a paragraph. In *Weaving It Together, Book 2*, you will learn how to write a good paragraph with a topic sentence. But at this point it is important for you just to follow the format.

1. Use lined paper.
2. Write your name, course number, and date in the upper right-hand corner.
3. Write a title in the center of the top of the page. Capitalize the first, last, and all important words in the title. Do not capitalize **the**, **a/an**, or *prepositions* unless they begin the title. Do not underline the title. Do not use a period.
4. Leave a one-inch margin on both sides of the page. Do not write in the left-hand margin.
5. Indent the first line of every paragraph.
6. Write on every other line of the paper.
7. Capitalize the first word in each sentence and end each sentence with a period.

The following list will help you check paragraph form:

Checklist

_____ Did you indent the first line?

_____ Did you give a title to your sentences?

_____ Did you write the title with a capital letter?

_____ Did you put the title in the center of the top of the page?

_____ Did you write on every other line?

3. Edit your work.

Work with a partner or your teacher to edit your sentences. Correct spelling, punctuation, vocabulary, and grammar.

4. Write your final copy.

Circle T if the sentence is true. Circle F if the sentence is false.

1. On New Year's Day in Madagasgar, everyone pours water over his/her head.   T   F

2. Ten million people have the same birthday as you.   T   F

3. Canadians celebrate Thanksgiving on the same day as in the United States.   T   F

4. The British celebrate Thanksgiving on the fourth Thursday in November.   T   F

5. In early May in Japan, men fly kites to celebrate the birth of their first-born sons.   T   F

6. Father's Day is an official holiday in the United States, and people do not work on this day.   T   F

7. The British celebrate Independence Day on July 4.   T   F

8. At an American wedding, people throw rice on the bride.   T   F

UNIT 2

Places

Chapter 3: Hollywood

PRE-READING QUESTIONS

Discuss these questions with your classmates or teacher.

1 What does Hollywood make you think of?

2 What are some special things to see in Hollywood?

3 Where do American movie stars live today?

Reading: Hollywood

When we think of Hollywood, we think of **movies** and famous **movie stars**. They are part of Hollywood's history. Today people make movies in other places too. Not all famous movie stars live in Hollywood. But Hollywood is still a very special city in Los Angeles, California.

You can easily see where Hollywood is in Los Angeles. There is a big **sign** on the **hills**. It says "HOLLYWOOD." The white letters are fifty feet tall. You can see the sign from **far away**. The Hollywood sign is a famous **landmark** in Los Angeles. Many postcards show this famous Hollywood landmark.

In the hills of Hollywood, there is also the Hollywood Bowl. This is an open-air theater. It is one of the largest open-air theaters in the world. It has seventeen thousand **seats** and a very special **stage**. The **design** of the stage was by the great American **architect** Frank Lloyd Wright. You can listen to all kinds of concerts at the Hollywood Bowl.

VOCABULARY

Complete the definition. Circle the letter of the correct answer.

1. Moving pictures or films that you may see in a cinema or theater are called _____.
    a. movies
    b. letter

2. Another name for an actor in a film is a _____.
    a. movie star
    b. postcard

3. A mark that represents something is a _____.
    a. city
    b. sign

4. Land that is not high as a mountain is called a _____.
    a. hill
    b. theater

5. Someone who lives _____ from you does not live near you.
    a. open-air
    b. far away

6. Something that you can recognize easily, such as a tall building, is a _____.
    a. letter
    b. landmark

7. The place where you sit is called a _____.
    a. seat
    b. theater

8. The place where actors, musicians, or singers perform in a theater is called a _____.
    a. landmark
    b. stage

9. The plan of a building is called the _____.

    a. design

    b. bowl

10. A person who makes plans for buildings is called _____

    a. a movie star

    b. an architect

A. Looking for the Main Ideas

Circle the letter of the best answer.

1. Today Hollywood is _____.

    a. a special city in Los Angeles

    b. where all the movie stars live

    c. where they make all the movies

2. You can see where Hollywood is in Los Angeles because _____

    a. it is a hill

    b. postcards show you

    c. there is a big sign on the hills

3. The Hollywood Bowl is

    a. a place where you see movies

    b. one of the largest open-air theaters in the world

    c. a hill in Hollywood

B. Looking for Details

One word in each sentence is not correct. Rewrite the sentence with the correct word.

1. There is a big star on the hills, which says "HOLLYWOOD."

    _____

    _____

2. The white landmarks of the sign are fifty feet tall.

    _____

    _____

3. The Hollywood sign has seventeen thousand seats.

    _____

    _____

4. The Hollywood Bowl is a special landmark.

_____

_____

5. The design of the stage was by the great Hollywood architect
   Frank Lloyd Wright.

_____

_____

6. The Hollywood Bowl is an open-air hill.

_____

_____

DISCUSSION

Discuss these questions with your classmates.

1. Describe a special place (building, park, etc.) in the city where you
   are now.
2. Describe a special place in another city or town you know.
3. What city or place do you want to visit one day? Say why.

Adjectives

Words that describe nouns are called adjectives. *They usually answer the question "What kind?"*

Examples:

> There is a big   sign on the hills.
>   (Adj.) (Noun)
> The sign is a famous landmark.
>   (Adj.)   (Noun)

Adjectives are the same form if you use them with a singular noun or a plural noun.

Examples:

> There are big letters.
>   (Adj.) (Pl. noun)
> Hollywood has some famous landmarks.
>   (Adj.) (Pl. noun)

Adjectives come before nouns.

Examples:

> There is a **big** sign.
> Not all **famous** movie stars live in Hollywood.

Adjectives can also come after the verb "to be."

Examples:

> Hollywood is **famous.**
> The stage of the Hollywood Bowl is **special.**

Exercise 1

Underline the adjectives in the sentences.

1. Hollywood is a special city in Los Angeles.
2. You can see the white letters from far away.
3. That sign is a famous landmark.
4. The Hollywood Bowl is an open-air theater.
5. The Hollywood Bowl has a special stage.

Put the words in the correct order.

Example:

Hollywood/city/is/a/special

Hollywood is a special city.

1. The/white/are/letters

2. City/is/a/Hollywood/famous

3. Frank Lloyd Wright/architect/was/famous/a

4. Postcards/the famous/show/landmark

Exercise 3

Write about what you think. Write complete sentences. Use an adjective in each sentence.

1. What is the town you are living in now like?

   _____

   _____

2. Describe a special place in your town.

   _____

   _____

3. What is your school like?

   _____

   _____

4. What is your class like?

   _____

   _____

1. Write sentences.

Answer these questions with complete sentences.

a. Name a city that is special for you.

_____

_____

b. Where is this city?

_____

_____

c. Describe this city using one or two adjectives.

_____

_____

d. Name one thing this city has that is special. Describe it using adjectives.

_____

_____

e. Name and describe a special building in this city.

_____

_____

2. Rewrite in paragraph form.

Rewrite your sentences in the form of a paragraph (see page 19).

Checklist

_____ Did you indent the first line?

_____ Did you give a title to your sentences? (Use the name of the city.)

_____ Did you put the title in the center of the top of the page?

_____ Did you write on every other line?

3. **Edit your work.**

Work with a partner or your teacher to edit your sentences. Check spelling, punctuation, vocabulary, and grammar.

4. **Write your final copy.**

Chapter 4: Mexico

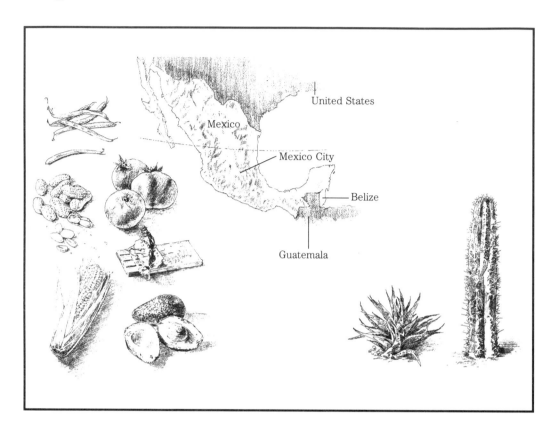

PRE-READING QUESTIONS

Discuss these questions with your classmates or teacher.

1. Name some countries around Mexico.

2. What foods and plants come from Mexico?

3. What cities do you know in Mexico?

4. What other things do you know about Mexico?

Reading: Mexico

Mexico's **neighbors** are the United States to the north and Guatemala and Belize to the south. Mexico is about one **quarter** of the size of the United States. Mexico has more than ninety million people. The language of Mexico is Spanish. This makes Mexico the world's largest Spanish-speaking country.

Mexico City is the **capital** and largest city of Mexico. The city is also very high. It is 7,349 feet high (2,240 meters). This makes it one of the highest capital cities in the world. The **population** of Mexico City grows bigger every day. About thirty million people live there. It has more people than any other city in the world, even more than Tokyo.

Mexico also has its special plants. Many of the foods we eat started in Mexico. Foods like beans, **maize**, avocados, tomatoes, peanuts, chili peppers, **vanilla**, and chocolate come from Mexico. Mexico is also famous for its **cactus** plants. Mexico has more kinds of cactus than any other country!

Circle the letter of the word which correctly completes the sentence.

1. The United States is Mexico's _____.

    a. neighbor

    b. country

2. Twenty-five percent or 1/4 is another way of saying a _____.

    a. meter

    b. quarter

3. Mexico City is the _____ of Mexico.

    a. capital

    b. people

4. Mexico City has a _____ of thirty million people.

    a. language

    b. population

5. Many foods come from Mexico. _____ is a kind of corn from Mexico.

    a. Maize

    b. Chocolate

6. Chocolate ice cream is brown in color, and _____ ice cream is white.

    a. tomato

    b. vanilla

7. Mexico is famous for _____ plants, which grow in hot places like deserts.

    a. cactus

    b. city

A. Looking for the Main Ideas

Write complete answers to these questions.

1. What countries are Mexico's neighbors?

2. What is the capital city of Mexico?

3. What foods started in Mexico?

B. Looking for Details

Circle T if the sentence is true. Circle F if the sentence is false.

1. Mexico has a quarter of a million people.   T F
2. The language of Mexico is not Spanish.   T F
3. Mexico City is one of the highest capital cities in the world. T F
4. Tokyo has more people than Mexico City.   T F
5. Mexico has the most kinds of cactus.   T F
6. Chocolate started in Mexico.   T F

DISCUSSION

Find students in your class not from your country. Then fill out the questionnaire below.

Country	Population	Name of Capital	Language	Special Things (foods/plant)
Mexico	90 million	Mexico City	Spanish	corn, beans, cactus

Now talk about a country from your questionnaire. Discuss these questions with your classmates.

1. What plants or animals are special to your country?
2. What is special about the capital of your country?
3. What special places does your country have?

The Comparative of Adjectives

When you want to compare two things that are different, use the comparative form of adjectives.

To form the comparative, we add **-er** to the adjective and put **than** after the adjective.

Examples:

Mexico is small**er than** the United States.
Mexico's population is big**ger than** the population of Tokyo.

Notes: If the adjective ends in one consonant and there is one vowel before it, double the consonant.
(big – bigger, hot – hotter)

If the adjective ends in **-y**, change **y** to **i** and add **-er**. Then put **than** after the adjective.
(happy – happier, easy – easier)

When the adjective has two syllables or more, put **more** in front of the adjective and **than** after the adjective.

Examples:

Tokyo is **more** expensive **than** Mexico City.
Tokyo is **more** crowded **than** Paris.

| Exercise 1 |

Give the number of syllables in each adjective. Then write the comparative form.

	Syllables	**Comparative Form**
1. beautiful	3	*more beautiful*
2. wet	____	_____
3. dry	____	_____
4. expensive	____	_____
5. old	____	_____
6. dangerous	____	_____
7. high	____	_____
8. large	____	_____

Complete each sentence with the comparative form of the adjectives in parentheses.

1. Mexico is (big) Guatamala.

   _____

   _____

2. Mexico is (small) the United States.

   _____

   _____

3. The Pacific Ocean is (large) the Atlantic Ocean.

   _____

   _____

4. The Sears Tower in Chicago is (tall) the Empire State Building.

   _____

   _____

5. The Nile River is (long) the Mississippi.

   _____

   _____

6. Mexico is (dry) Canada.

   _____

   _____

7. The Taj Mahal is (beautiful) the Sears Tower.

   _____

   _____

8. Paris is (expensive) Mexico City.

   _____

   _____

The Superlative of Adjectives

When you want to compare more than two things, use the superlative form of adjectives.

To form the superlative, add **-est** to the end of the adjective.

Examples:

Mexico City is the larg**est** city of Mexico.

Mexico City is the high**est** capital city.

When the adjective has two syllables or more, add **the most** in front of the adjective.

Examples:

Mexico City is **the most** crowded city in the world.

Mexico City is **the most** popular city in Mexico.

Exercise 3

Complete each sentence with the superlative form of the adjective in parentheses.

1. Mexico is (large) Spanish-speaking country in the world.

   Mexico is the largest Spanish-speaking country in the world.

2. Alaska is (big) state in the United States.

3. Vatican City is (small) country in the world.

4. Mount Everest is (high) mountain in the world.

5. The Nile is (long) river in the world.

6. Death Valley in California is (hot) place in the United States.

_____

_____

7. Tokyo is one of (expensive) cities in the world.

_____

_____

8. Acapulco in Mexico is (popular) city in Mexico for tourists.

_____

_____

Exercise 4

Write about what you think. Use complete sentences.

1. Which is the most interesting city for you?

_____

_____

2. Which is the most dangerous place?

_____

_____

3. Which is the most beautiful place?

_____

_____

4. Which is the largest city in your country?

_____

_____

1. Write sentences.

Answer these questions with complete sentences.

a. Which country do you come from?

_____

_____

b. Where is your country? (Give the names of neighboring countries.)

_____

_____

c. What is the population of your country?

_____

_____

d. What language(s) do most people speak?

_____

_____

e. What is the capital city of your country? Is it also the largest city?
(If not, tell which city is the largest.)

_____

_____

f. What special things does your country have? (Name special
plants/foods/animals.)

_____

_____

g. What can you say about your country, using a superlative adjective? (**Example**: My country is the most beautiful country in the world.)

_____

_____

2. Rewrite in paragraph form.

Rewrite your sentences in the form of a paragraph.

Checklist

_____ Did you indent the first line?

_____ Did you give a title to your sentences?

_____ Did you write the title with a capital letter?

_____ Did you put the title in the center of the top of the page?

_____ Did you write on every other line?

3. Edit your work.

Work with a partner or your teacher to edit your sentences. Correct spelling, punctuation, vocabulary, and grammar.

4. Write your final copy.

Test your knowledge. Circle the correct answer.

1. The largest city in the world in area is _____.

    a. London, England

    b. New York, U.S.A.

    c. Mount Isa, Australia

2. The oldest capital city in the world is _____.

    a. Rome, Italy

    b. Damascus, Syria

    c. Athens, Greece

3. The world's largest palace is _____.

    a. The Imperial Palace, Beijing

    b. Versailles, France

    c. Buckingham Palace, London

4. The South Pole is _____.

    a. warmer than the North Pole

    b. colder than the North Pole

    c. the same temperature as the North Pole

5. The highest and lowest points in the United States are both in the state of _____.

    a. California

    b. Colorado

    c. Arizona

6. The name "El Pueblo de Nuestra Señora la Reine de los Angeles de Porciuncola" was the original name of _____.

    a. California

    b. the cathedral in Mexico City

    c. Los Angeles

UNIT 3

Health

Chapter 5: Sleep

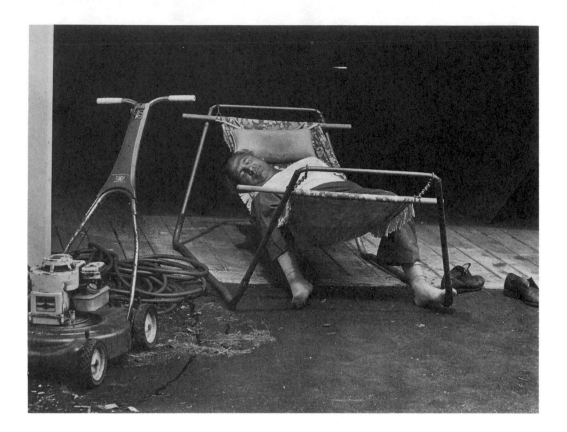

PRE-READING QUESTIONS:

1 How much sleep do we need?

2 Do many people have problems falling asleep?

3 What do you do when you can't sleep?

Reading: Sleep

How much sleep do we need? We are all different. Some people need only three hours of sleep a night. Others need ten hours of sleep a night. Most Americans sleep an **average** of seven to eight hours a night. After age fifty, the average sleep time goes down to 6.5 hours a night.

Most people have a night when they cannot sleep. About one in three Americans has a problem with sleep. Many of these people cannot **fall asleep**. The name of this problem is **insomnia**.

This is not a new problem. Many famous people in history had insomnia. Some of these people had special ideas to make them sleep. Benjamin Franklin, the famous **statesman** and **inventor**, had four beds. He moved from one to the other to fall asleep. King Louis XIV of France had 413 beds and hoped to fall asleep in one of them. Mark Twain, the famous American **author,** had a different way. He lay on his side across the end of the bed!

Complete the definitions. Circle the letter of the correct answer.

1. The middle point between a high number and a low number is the _____.

    a. idea

    b. average

2. When you close your eyes and begin to sleep, you _____.

    a. have insomnia

    b. fall asleep

3. When a person has a problem with sleep, the name of the problem is _____.

    a. history

    b. insomnia

4. A man who is a leader in politics is _____.

    a. an author

    b. a statesman

5. A person who gets an idea for something for the first time is _____.

    a. an inventor

    b. an American

6. The writer of a book is the _____.

    a. inventor

    b. author

COMPREHENSION

A. Looking for the Main Ideas

Circle the letter of the correct answer.

1. Most Americans sleep _____.
    a. three hours
    b. ten hours
    c. seven to eight hours

2. People who have a problem with sleep _____.
    a. are Americans
    b. are famous
    c. have insomnia

3. Benjamin Franklin, King Louis XIV of France, and Mark Twain all had _____.
    a. insomnia
    b. four beds
    c. no ideas

B. Looking for Details

Circle T if the sentence is true. Circle F if the sentence is false.

1. Some people need only three hours of sleep a night.   T   F
2. After age fifty, the average sleep time is 5.5 hours a night.   T   F
3. One in four Americans has a problem with sleep.   T   F
4. Many famous people in history had insomnia.   T   F
5. Benjamin Franklin had four beds.   T   F
6. Mark Twain was a famous statesman.   T   F

Find out from the students in your class how they sleep. Fill out the questionnaire below.

Name	Number of Hours	Get Up in the Night	Dream
Klara	9	sometimes	no

Discuss these questions with your classmates.

1. What kinds of things do people eat or drink to help them sleep?
2. What kinds of things make you sleep badly or lose sleep?
3. What things do you need in a room to be able to sleep?

WRITING SKILLS

Using *when*

We use **when** *to show that two things happen at the same time. Notice the use of the comma when the sentence starts with* **when**.

Examples:

I have the lights on when I sleep.
or
When I sleep, I have the lights on.

Extra Vocabulary for *Sleep*

> **to snore** = the noise you make when you sleep
> **to dream** = the pictures you see in your sleep
> **a nightmare** = a bad dream

Exercise 1

Join the two sentences with **when**. *Begin your sentence with* **when**. *Use the correct punctuation.*

1. I sleep. I have the radio on.

   _____

   _____

2. I sleep. I snore.

   _____

   _____

3. I sleep. I move about a lot.

   _____

   _____

4. I sleep. I like to hold something.

   _____

   _____

5. I sleep. I lie on my side.

_____

_____

6. I have problems. I cannot sleep.

_____

_____

7. I eat too much. I have a nightmare.

_____

_____

8. I am in a different bed. I cannot sleep.

_____

_____

WRITING PRACTICE

1. Write sentences.

Answer these questions with complete sentences.

a. How much sleep do you need?

_____

_____

b. What time do you usually go to bed, and what time do you get up in the morning?

_____

_____

c. Are the lights in your room on or off when you sleep? Is the window open or closed? Is your room quiet, or is there noise?

_____

_____

d. How often do you wake up in the middle of the night? Every day or sometimes? What do you do when you wake up?

_____

_____

e. How do you usually sleep? On your back, side, or stomach? Do you move about a lot?

_____

_____

2. Rewrite in paragraph form.

Rewrite your sentences in the form of a paragraph.

Checklist

_____ Did you indent the first line?

_____ Did you give a title to your sentences?

_____ Did you write the title with a capital letter?

_____ Did you put the title in the center of the top of the page?

_____ Did you write on every other line?

3. Edit your work.

Work with a partner or your teacher to edit your sentences. Correct spelling, punctuation, vocabulary, and grammar.

4. Write your final copy.

Chapter 6: Laughter

PRE-READING QUESTIONS

Discuss these questions with your classmates or teacher.

1 Describe the people in the picture.

2 What well-known funny people do you know in your country?

3 How do you feel after you laugh?

Reading: Laughter

Some people say that laughter is the best medicine. Scientists are beginning to agree with this. They are studying laughter seriously and are finding it is really good for us.

So what happens when we laugh? We use fifteen different **muscles** in our face, and laughing is good for every **organ** in our body. When we laugh, we breathe quickly and exercise the face, shoulders, and chest. Our **blood pressure** goes down, and our **circulation** gets better. Our **heartbeat** is lower and our **brain** makes a natural **painkiller** called a beta-endorphin.

Every minute we laugh is the same as forty-five minutes of **relaxation**. Many doctors around the world believe that laughter helps us get better when we are sick.

Of course, there are many kinds of laughter. We may change the way we laugh in different situations. But we all have a laugh that is special to us. How do you usually laugh?

Complete the sentences with the correct word.

1. When we laugh, we use fifteen different _____ in our face.

    a. pain killers

    b. muscles

2. Laughter is good for every _____ in our body.

    a. organ

    b. face

3. When we laugh, our _____ goes down.

    a. blood pressure

    b. brain

4. Laughter makes our _____ better.

    a. medicine

    b. circulation

5. A beta-endorphin is   .

    a. an exercise

    b. a natural painkiller

6. Laughter makes our _____ lower.

    a. chest

    b. heartbeat

7. Laughter makes a natural painkiller in our _____.

    a. shoulders

    b. brain

8. Forty-five minutes of _____ is the same as one minute of laughter.

    a. relaxation

    b. circulation

COMPREHENSION

A. Looking for the Main Ideas

Circle the letter of the correct answer.

1. Scientists say that laughter _____.

    a. is good for us

    b. is serious

    c. is not really good

2. Laughter is good for _____.

    a. our body

    b. only the face

    c. only the chest and shoulders

3. Many doctors believe that laughter _____.

    a. helps us get better when we are sick

    b. makes us sick

    c. does not help

B. Looking for Details

One word in each sentence is not correct. Rewrite the sentence with the correct word.

1. We use fifty different muscles in our face.

    _____

    _____

2. Laughing is good for every different organ in our brain.

    _____

    _____

3. Every minute we laugh is the same as forty-five hours of relaxation.

    _____

    _____

4. We may change the way we laugh in different shoulders.

_____

_____

5. When we laugh, we breathe seriously.

_____

_____

6. Our face makes a natural painkiller.

_____

_____

DISCUSSION

Find out how the students in your class laugh.

1. How many students laugh with their mouths open?
2. How many students in class laugh loudly?
3. How many students have a shy and quiet laugh?
4. How many students never laugh?

Adverbs

An **adverb** tells you something about a verb. It answers the question "How?" It usually comes after the verb.

Example:

When we laugh, we breathe quickly
            (Verb) (Adv.)

We form an adverb by adding **-ly** to an adjective

Example:

Adjective	Adverb
loud	loudly
quiet	quietly

Exercise 1

Change the adjectives in parentheses into adverbs and rewrite the sentences.

1. She laughs (free).

   _____

   _____

2. He laughs (loud).

   _____

   _____

3. She laughs (shy).

   _____

   _____

4. He laughs (nervous).

   _____

   _____

5. They are studying (serious).

   _____

   _____

6. He speaks (quiet).

_____

_____

Exercise 2

Write five sentences about yourself, using these adverbs:
quickly   slowly   quietly   loudly   seriously

1. _____

_____

2. _____

_____

3. _____

_____

4. _____

_____

5. _____

_____

Extra Vocabulary for **Laughter**

a joke = something that you say or do that makes people laugh
to be embarrassed = to feel uncomfortable because of something

1. Write sentences.

Answer these questions with complete sentences.

a. Choose one of the following sentences and copy it below.

I like to laugh a lot.

I don't like to laugh.

I sometimes laugh.

_____

b. What things make you laugh (jokes, funny situations, when you are

embarrassed, etc.)?

_____

_____

c. When did you laugh last?

_____

_____

d. What happened? Whom were you with? Where were you?

_____

_____

e. Did you laugh quietly or loudly?

_____

_____

f. Do you feel like laughing when you think of this situation?

_____

_____

2. Rewrite in paragraph form.

Rewrite your sentences in the form of a paragraph.

Checklist

_____ Did you indent the first line?

_____ Did you give a title to your sentences?

_____ Did you write the title with a capital letter?

_____ Did you put the title in the center of the top of the page?

_____ Did you write on every other line?

3. Edit your work.

Work with a partner or your teacher to edit your sentences. Correct spelling, punctuation, vocabulary, and grammar.

4. Write your final copy.

Circle T if the sentence is true. Circle F if the sentence is false.

1. You use seventy-two muscles to say one word.   T   F
2. It takes five seconds for blood to go all around your body.   T   F
3. The color of your blood inside your body is blue.   T   F
4. You can't sneeze with your eyes open.   T   F
5. When you start to cry, you feel worse.   T   F
6. Your hair grows faster at night.   T   F

UNIT 4

Customs

Chapter 7: A Baby's
First Haircut

PRE-READING QUESTIONS

Discuss these questions with your classmates or teacher.

1 What special day do you think they are celebrating?

2 What special days for children do you have in your country?

3 How do people celebrate those days in your country?

Reading: A Baby's First Haircut

The natives of Peru and Bolivia have a special custom for a baby. They **celebrate** the baby's first haircut with a fiesta. At the fiesta there is lots of food, music, and dancing.

The parents do not cut the baby's hair for a few years. They **invite** relatives and friends to the fiesta.

On this special day the baby sits on a high chair like a king or queen. Then the **godmother** separates the baby's hair into **locks**. The number of locks is the same as the number of guests at the fiesta. The godmother then **ties** each lock with a pretty **ribbon**.

The **godfather** cuts the first lock. He also says what **gift** he is giving. The gifts may be an animal, a piece of land, or a lot of money. After him, each guest cuts off a lock and makes a gift of money. The money can pay for the fiesta, or the parents can save the money for the baby's future.

VOCABULARY

Rewrite each sentence, replacing the underlined words with one of the words below.

celebrate	invite	godmother	ribbon
locks	ties	godfather	gift

1. The natives of Peru and Bolivia <u>have a party</u> on the day of a baby's first haircut.

   _____

   _____

2. The parents <u>ask</u> relatives and friends to the fiesta.

   _____

3. The <u>woman who takes responsibility for a person at baptism</u> separates the baby's hair.

   _____

   _____

4. The number of <u>small pieces of hair</u> is the same as the number of guests.

   _____

5. The godmother <u>joins together with a narrow band</u> each lock.

   _____

6. She ties each lock with a <u>narrow band of silk or other material</u>.

   _____

7. The <u>man who takes responsibility for a person at baptism</u> may give a lot of money, an animal, or a piece of land.

   _____

   _____

8. Each guest gives a <u>present</u> of money.

_____

A. Looking for the Main Ideas

Write complete answers to these questions.

1. What do the Indians of Peru and Bolivia celebrate?

_____

2. Who separates the baby's hair into locks?

_____

3. What does the godfather do?_____

B. Looking for Details

Circle T if the sentence is true. Circle F if the sentence is false.

1. At the fiesta there is food, music, and dancing.	T	F
2. The baby sits on an animal.	T	F
3. The number of locks is the same as the number of guests.	T	F
4. The godfather ties each lock with a ribbon.	T	F
5. Each guest cuts a lock and gives a gift of money.	T	F
6. The money pays for the godfather's future.	T	F

Discuss these questions with your classmates.

1. Do you think it is better to give gifts or money to a child on his/her special day?
2. Why is it important to celebrate special days for children or young people?
3. How long do you think a celebration should last (a few hours, one day, one week)?

Count Nouns and Noncount Nouns

Count nouns are nouns that can be counted.
Noncount nouns are nouns that cannot be counted.
When we use a **count noun**

    1. We can put a/an in front of it.

Example:

    They invite a friend.

    2. It has a plural form.

Example:

    They invite friends

    3. We can put a number in front of it.

Example:

    one friend, two friends

When we use a **noncount noun**

    1. We cannot put a/an in front of a noncount noun.

Example:

    There is music.

    2. It usually does not have a plural form.

Example:

    There is lots of music.

    3. We cannot put a number in front of it.

We can use **lots of**, or **a lot of** before both a count noun and a noncount noun.

There are many noncount nouns in English. Here are some of them. You may add other noncount nouns to the list.

Materials/Food	Abstract Nouns	Activities/Subjects	General Nouns
food	luck	dancing	money
fruit	happiness	music	jewelry
gold	love	singing	clothing
hair	fun	homework	furniture
corn	intelligence	grammar	mail
salt	advice	work	cash

*Note: *Food*, *fruit*, and *hair* can also be count nouns.

Now underline all the noncount nouns in the reading.

Exercise 1

Look at the underlined noun in each sentence. Circle C if it is a count noun. Circle NC if it is a noncount noun.

1.	There is lots of <u>food</u>.	C	NC
2.	She has a <u>haircut</u>.	C	NC
3.	How many <u>locks</u> does she have?	C	NC
4.	They invite <u>relatives</u>.	C	NC
5.	Each one has a <u>ribbon</u>.	C	NC
6.	There is <u>music</u>.	C	NC
7.	They can save the <u>money</u>.	C	NC
8.	He gave her a piece of <u>land</u>.	C	NC
9.	She gets lots of <u>gifts</u>.	C	NC
10.	They have a <u>custom</u>.	C	NC
11.	We have a lot of <u>fruit</u>.	C	NC
12.	She wore beautiful <u>jewelry</u>.	C	NC

Write **a**, **an**, or **some** in front of each word.

1. We have _____ gift.

2. They have _____ food.

3. She has _____ dollar.

4. He has _____ animal.

5. We see _____ people.

6. They give _____ gold.

7. I listen to _____ music.

8. I have _____ idea.

Exercise 3

Make sentences using the following words.

1. food = We have a lot of food at the party.

2. money = _____

_____

3. music = _____

_____

4. dancing = _____

_____

1. Write sentences.

Answer these questions with complete sentences.

a. What is the name of a special day in your country (name day, sixteenth birthday, etc.)?

_____

_____

b. What day or days do they celebrate it?

_____

_____

c. Is it a religious day or some other kind of day?

_____

_____

d. What do people do on this day?

   • Do people wear special clothes?

   • Do they have a party at home, or do they go out?

   • Do they cook a lot of food?

   • Is there music and/or dancing?

   • Do people bring gifts? If so, what kind?

_____

_____

_____

e. Why is this day important?

_____

_____

2. Rewrite in paragraph form.

Rewrite your sentences in the form of a paragraph.

Checklist

_____ Did you indent the first line?

_____ Did you give a title to your sentence?

_____ Did you write the title with a capital letter?

_____ Did you put the title in the center of the top of the page?

_____ Did you write on every other line?

3. Edit your work.

Work with a partner or your teacher to edit your sentences. Correct spelling, punctuation, vocabulary, and grammar.

4. Write your final copy.

Chapter 8: Dinner Customs in Ghana

....

Discuss these questions with your classmates or teacher.

1 Describe how the people in the picture are eating.

2 In what countries do people not use forks and knives for eating? What do they use?

3 What time do you usually invite a guest to dinner in your country?

Reading: Dinner Customs in Ghana

Dinner customs are different around the world. If you are a dinner guest in Ghana, this information will help you.

In Ghana dinner is usually from four in the afternoon to six in the evening. But there are no **strict rules** about time in Ghana. Whenever a guest arrives, a family **offers** food.

When you go to a home, the **host** takes you to the living room first. At this time everyone welcomes you. Then you go to the dining room. There you wash your hands in a **bowl** of water. All the food is on the table.

In Ghana you usually eat with your fingers. You eat from the same **dish** as everyone else. But you eat from one side of the dish only. It is not **polite** to get food from the other side of the dish. After dinner, you wash your hands again in a bowl of water.

Most meals in Ghana have a dish called fufu. People in Ghana make fufu from the powder of some plants. Sometimes they cut the fufu with a **saw** because it is very hard and like **rubber**. You must **chew** fufu well, or you can get sick. You eat fufu with the fingers of your right hand only.

What is the meaning of the underlined words? Circle the letter of the correct answer.

1. There are no <u>strict</u> rules about time.

    a. strange

    b. strong

2. A family <u>offers</u> food.

    a. gives

    b. buys

3. The <u>host</u> takes you to the living room.

    a. oldest person

    b. person who receives guests

4. You wash your hands in a <u>bowl</u> of water.

    a. round container for liquids

    b. very large square container

5. You eat from the same <u>dish</u>.

    a. round table

    b. round plate for holding food

6. It is not <u>polite</u> to get food from the other side of the dish.

    a. bad manners

    b. good manners

7. They cut fufu with a <u>saw</u>.

    a. small knife

    b. tooling for cutting hard material like wood

8. Fufu is like <u>rubber</u>.

    a. elastic

    b. wood

9. You must <u>chew</u> fufu well.

    a. crush with your teeth

    b. dry

A. Looking for the Main Ideas

Circle the letter of the correct answer.

1. In Ghana _____.

     a. dinner is always at six

     b. rules for time are not strict

     c. a family offers food only at four

2. People in Ghana eat _____.

     a. from one side of a dish to the other

     b. from the other side of the dish

     c. with their fingers

3. Most dishes in Ghana _____.

     a. have a dish called fufu

     b. do not have fufu

     c. are like rubber

B. Looking for Details

One word in each sentence is not correct. Rewrite the sentence with the correct word.

1. The host takes you to the dining room first.

     _____

     _____

2. You wash your hands in a dish of water.

     _____

     _____

3. It is not polite to get food from the same side of the dish.

     _____

     _____

4. People in Ghana cut fufu in a saw.

_____

_____

5. You must cut fufu well, or you can get sick.

_____

_____

6. You eat fufu with your left hand only.

_____

_____

DISCUSSION

Discuss these questions with your classmates.

1. How are dinner customs in the United States different from those in your country?
2. How many kinds of dishes do you usually have for dinner in your country?
3. What is not polite at the table in your country?

Prepositional Phrases

A **phrase** is a group of words that is part of a sentence. A **prepositional phrase** begins with a preposition. The preposition always has an object. The **object of the preposition** can be a noun or a pronoun.

Examples:

> You eat with your fingers.
>   (Prep.) (O. of prep.)

> People cut the fish with a saw.
>   (Prep.)(O. of prep.)

Sometimes there is more than one prepositional phrase.

Example:

> You eat from one side of the dish.
>   (Prep. phrase) (Prep. pharase)

Sometimes a prepositional phrase can come at the beginning of a sentence.

Example:

> After dinner, you wash your hands.
> (Prep. phrase)

The following are some common prepositions:

about	at	down	of	to
above	before	during	on	under
across	behind	for	out	until
after	below	from	over	up
against	beside	in	since	with
among	between	into	through	without
around	by	near	till	

Exercise 1

Find the prepositional phrase (PP) in these sentences.

1. You wash your hands in a bowl.
                         PP

2. The host takes you to the living room.

3. At this time, everyone welcomes you.

4. The food is on the table.

5. Most dishes in Ghana have fufu.

6. Most people eat from the same dish.

Exercise 2

Complete the sentences with the correct preposition.

1. They put all the food _____ the table.

2. We eat _____ a knife and fork.

3. We have dinner _____ seven in the evening.

4. We put the soup _____ a bowl.

5. We have dinner _____ the dinner room.

6. In my country, it is not polite to eat _____ fingers.

1. Write sentences.

Write complete answers to these questions.

a. What time do you usually have dinner in your country?

_____

_____

b. What is on the table (bowls, glasses, cups, different kinds of food, bread, rice)?

_____

_____

c. What does each person have (a bowl, a plate, a napkin, etc.)?

_____

_____

d. What do you eat with?

_____

_____

e. What do you eat?

_____

_____

f. What is not polite at the table in your country?

_____

_____

2. Rewrite in paragraph form.

Rewrite your sentences in the form of a paragraph.

Checklist

_____ Did you indent the first line?

_____ Did you give a title to your sentences?

_____ Did you write the title with a capital letter?

_____ Did you put the title in the center of the top of the page?

_____ Did you write on every other line?

3. Edit your work.

Work with a partner or your teacher to edit your sentences. Correct spelling, punctuation, vocabulary, and grammar.

4. Write your final copy.

DO YOU KNOW THESE INTERESTING CUSTOMS?

Circle T if the answer is true. Circle F if the answer is false.

1. The ancient Romans used to break a cake over the head of a bride to bring happiness.   T   F

2. In Fiji, to show respect to someone, you fold your arms in front of you.   T   F

3. In Sweden it is a custom to eat with the fork in the right hand.   T   F

4. In Iceland the names in a telephone book are first names instead of last names.   T   F

5. In Scotland it is OK to eat on the street.   T   F

6. It is a custom in France for the man to offer his hand first when a man and woman meet.   T   F

7. When an Inuit tells friends a funny story, he/she turns his/her back and faces the wall.   T   F

UNIT 5

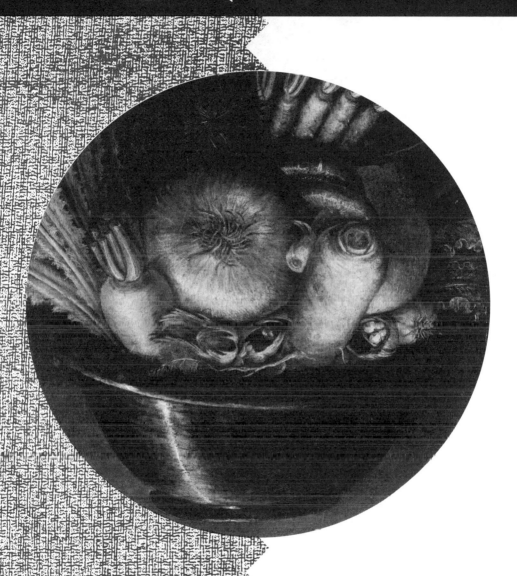

Food

Chapter 9: Chocolate

....

Discuss these questions with your classmates or teacher.

1 How often do you eat chocolate?

2 What kinds of foods can have chocolate in them?

3 Do you think chocolate is good for you?

Reading: Chocolate

The Aztecs of Mexico knew about chocolate a long time ago. They made it into a drink. Sometimes they put **hot chili peppers** with the chocolate. They called the drink "xocoatl" which means "**bitter** juice." This is where the word "chocolate" comes from.

The Spanish took the drink from the land of the Aztecs to Europe. The Spanish didn't like peppers so they **added** sugar to the chocolate. This drink became very popular in Europe. Until 1850 chocolate was only a drink. After that time Europeans **discovered** that chocolate was good to eat too.

The Aztecs believed that chocolate made you intelligent. Today, we do not believe this. But chocolate has a special **chemical**— phenylethylamine. This is the same chemical the body makes when a person is in love. Which do you prefer? Chocolate or being in love?

Complete the definitions. Circle the letter of the correct answer.

1. When peppers burn your mouth like fire, they are _____

    a. hot

    b. bitter

2. The kinds of peppers that are hot and burn your mouth are called _____.

    a. chocolate peppers

    b. chili peppers

3. Something that has a taste like strong coffee without sugar is _____.

    a. bitter

    b. popular

4. When you put something with something else, you _____ it.

    a. like

    b. add

5. When you find something that nobody knows before, you _____ it.

    a. believe

    b. discover

6. Phenylethylamine is a _____.

    a. chemical

    b. drink

A. Looking for the Main Ideas

Circle the letter of the best answer.

1. The Aztecs made _____.

   a. chili peppers into a drink

   b. chocolate into a drink

   c. chocolate peppers

2. The Spanish _____.

   a. discovered chocolate

   b. gave chocolate to the Aztecs

   c. took the chocolate drink to Europe

3. Chocolate _____.

   a. has a special chemical

   b. has no special chemicals

   c. makes you love chemicals

B. Looking for Details

Circle T if the sentence is true. Circle F if the sentence is false.

1. The Aztecs put sugar into the chocolate.	T	F
2. The word "chocolate" means "bitter juice."	T	F
3. The Spanish took peppers to Europe.	T	F
4. In 1850 people began to eat chocolate.	T	F
5. Chocolate makes you intelligent.	T	F
6. Phenylethylamine is the chemical in chocolate.	T	F

DISCUSSION

Discuss these questions with your classmates.

1. Why do you think people like chocolate?

2. What is the most popular kind of chocolate people buy in your country?

3. The Aztecs drank chocolate with spices like vanilla or chili peppers. What other kinds of things can you mix with chocolate?

4. How would you create a wonderful chocolate dish?

Instructions

When you write instructions, you must use exact words to describe each step. It is also important to give all the steps in the correct order.

Look at these pictures. Put them in the correct order. Then fill in the blanks with the words below the pictures.

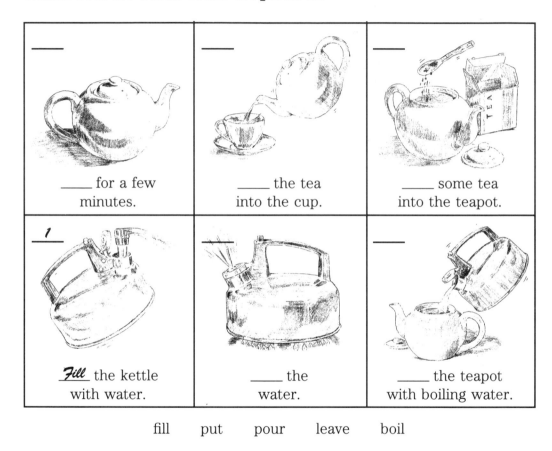

_____ for a few minutes.

_____ the tea into the cup.

_____ some tea into the teapot.

Fill the kettle with water.

_____ the water.

_____ the teapot with boiling water.

fill   put   pour   leave   boil

Exercise 1

Now write the complete sentences in the correct order.

1. _____

2. _____

3. _____

4. _____

5. _____

6. _____

Write six sentences to show how you make coffee or chocolate.

1. _____

2. _____

3. _____

4. _____

5. _____

6. _____

1. Write sentences.

Answer these questions with complete sentences.

1. Which drink do you like best: coffee, tea, or chocolate?

   _____

   _____

2. Do you drink this drink every day? How many times a day do you

   drink it?

   _____

   _____

3. When do you drink it?

   _____

   _____

4. What do you drink it in? What do you drink with it?

   _____

   _____

5. How do you make the drink?

   _____

   _____

6. How much do you like this drink? Can you live without it?

   _____

   _____

2. Rewrite in paragraph form.

Rewrite your sentences in the form of a paragraph.

Checklist

_____ Did you indent the first line?

_____ Did you give a title to your sentences?

_____ Did you write on every other line?

_____ Did you write the title with a capital letter?

_____ Did you put the title in the center of the top of the page?

_____ Did you write on every other line?

3. Edit your work.

Work with a partner or your teacher to edit your sentences. Correct spelling, punctuation, vocabulary, and grammar.

4. Write your final copy.

Chapter 10: Mustard

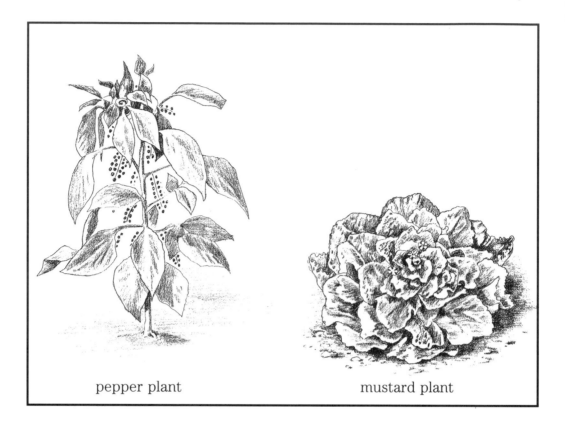

pepper plant   mustard plant

Discuss these questions with your classmates or teacher.

1 What spices do you know?

2 What do they smell or taste like?

3 What is your favorite spice?

Reading: Mustard

Mustard is a food that is three thousand years old. The **ancient** Egyptians and Chinese used it. Today the French must have it with beef. Americans like it on their hot dogs and hamburgers and often put it in sandwiches.

But mustard is famous not only as a food. For thousands of years people used mustard as medicine. In the United States people put mustard on their **chest** for a chest cold or used mustard for **rheumatism**. This kind of medicine is not so popular today.

The mustard plant is a pretty plant with bright yellow flowers. It grows easily everywhere. So how do we make this yellow **sauce** from it? We take the **seeds** of the plant. Then we **grind** the seeds and mix them with salt, **spices**, and vinegar. These spices are very important. Without them mustard will not have its bright yellow color.

Complete the definitions. Circle the letter of the correct answer.

1. When something is from a very long time ago, it is _____.
   a. Chinese
   b. ancient

2. The upper front part of your body, where you can find your heart and lungs, is the _____.
   a. beef
   b. chest

3. A kind of disease that gives pain to muscles and bones is _____.
   a. chest cold
   b. rheumatism

4. A thick liquid you put on food is a _____.
   a. sauce
   b. spice

5. The part of a plant that grows into a new plant is a _____.
   a. flower
   b. seed

6. When you make seeds into a powder, you _____ them.
   a. grind
   b. mix

A. Looking for the Main Ideas

Circle the letter of the best answer.

1. Mustard is _____.

    a. a new food

    b. an ancient food

    c. only a French food

2. Mustard is _____.

    a. also famous as medicine

    b. popular as medicine today

    c. not famous as a food

3. Mustard comes from _____.

    a. vinegar

    b. the seeds of the mustard plant

    c. yellow salt

B. Looking for Details

Circle T if the sentence is true. Circle F if the sentence is false.

1. Mustard is thirty thousand years old.	T	F
2. The Egyptians used it on hamburgers.	T	F
3. Mustard can be medicine.	T	F
4. People use mustard for chest colds.	T	F
5. Mustard plants grow only in China.	T	F
6. Spices give mustard its bright color.	T	F

garlic   soy sauce   curry

chili peppers   ginger   salt

DISCUSSION

Discuss these questions with your classmates.

1. What is the most popular spice in your country?
2. What is your favorite spice?
3. Which spices are good for you?
4. Which spices do you not like? Why?

WRITING SKILLS

Pronouns: it/them

It is a pronoun. A **pronoun** replaces another word so that you do not repeat the same word too many times.

1. Look back to the reading on *Mustard*.
2. Underline the pronoun **it** in the first paragraph.
3. How many times do you see the pronoun **it**?
4. What does the pronoun **it** replace?

We use the pronoun **it** for singular words.
We use the pronoun **them** for plural words.

Example:

Then we grind the seeds and mix **them** with salt.

Exercise 1

Replace the repeated word with the correct pronoun.

1. Jack loves mustard. He puts mustard on everything he eats.

   _____

   _____

2. I mix the spices together before I add the spices to the eggs.

   _____

   _____

3. My friend can't have too much salt in his food. He doesn't use salt in his cooking.

   _____

   _____

4. I put mustard on hot dogs and hamburgers, and I sometimes put mustard in sandwiches.

   _____

   _____

1. Write sentences.

Answer these questions with complete sentences.

a. What spice do you use the most?

(soy sauce, chili peppers, curry, salt, ginger, etc.)

_____

_____

b. What foods do you put it on?

(beef, fish, noodles, vegetables, etc.)

_____

_____

c. How many times a day do you eat foods with spices?

_____

_____

d. What special taste or smell do you like?

_____

_____

2. Rewrite in paragraph form.

Rewrite the sentences above in the form of a paragraph.

Checklist

_____ Did you indent the first line?

_____ Did you give a title to your sentences?

_____ Did you write the title with a capital letter?

_____ Did you put the title in the center of the top of the paper?

_____ Did you write on every other line?

3. Edit your work.

Work with a partner or your teacher to edit your sentences. Correct spelling, punctuation, vocabulary, and grammar.

4. Write your final copy.

FOOD QUIZ

Match the foods with the countries of their origin.

Germany ____   Ethiopia ____

Mexico ____   China ____

Austria ____   Ireland ____

1. ginger ale   2. chewing gum   3. coffee

4. spaghetti   5. croissant   6. hamburger

UNIT 6

Inventions

Chapter 11: Money

PRE-READING QUESTIONS

Discuss these questions with your classmates or teacher.

1 What color are paper bills in the United States? Are they all the same color?

2 Are all the paper bills in the United States the same size? Is this a good idea?

3 What names for money do you know? In which countries are they used?

Reading: Money

When we think of money, we think of **coins** and **paper bills**. That is what money is today. But in the past people used many things in place of money. Some countries used cows. Other countries used salt, tobacco, tea, or stones. Today there are still some places in the world that do not use paper money. One place is the **island** of Yap in the Pacific Ocean.

On the island of Yap, people use the heaviest money in the world—Yap stones. These are round, white stones with a hole in the middle. The Yap stones do not **originate from** the island. The Yap men have to go to islands four hundred miles away to **fetch** them. Big stones can be twelve feet high—as big as two **tall** men. Small stones are as big as a dinner plate.

Rich people do not carry the Yap stones. **Servants** follow the rich. Each servant carries a stone on a **pole** over his shoulder. Today the people on the island use paper money for everyday shopping. But for other things they still prefer Yap stones.

Rewrite each sentence, replacing the underlined words with one of the words or phrases below.

paper bills	coins	island	fetch
originate from	servants	tall	pole

1. We usually use two kinds of money. One kind is <u>money made of metal</u>.

   _____

   _____

2. The other kind is <u>money made of paper</u>.

   _____

   _____

3. The <u>land with water all around it</u> called Yap is in the Pacific Ocean.

   _____

   _____

4. The Yap stones do not <u>come from</u> this island.

   _____

   _____

5. The Yap men go 400 miles to <u>go and get</u> them.

   _____

   _____

6. The big Yap stones are as big as two <u>big</u> men.

   _____

   _____

7. People who work for the rich in their homes follow the rich.

_____

_____

8. Each servant carries a stone on a long stick.

_____

_____

A. Looking for the Main Ideas

Circle the letter of the best answer.

1. People _____.

   a. always use paper money and coins

   b. always used coins in the past

   c. still do not use paper money all the time

2. On the island of Yap, people use _____.

   a. stones as money

   b. two tall men as money

   c. small stones

3. People on the island of Yap _____.

   a. use Yap stones for everyday shopping

   b. still prefer Yap stones

   c. carry the rich on their shoulders

B. Looking for Details

Circle T if the sentence is true. Circle F if the sentence is false.

1. Yap stones have a hole in the middle.	T F
2. Yap stones originate from the island of Yap.	T F
3. Yap stones are all twelve feet high.	T F
4. People use small stones for dinner plates.	T F
5. Servants carry the Yap stones for the rich.	T F
6. A servant carries a stone on a pole on his shoulders.	T F

Find students not from your country. Then fill out the questionnaire below.

Name	Country	Name of Money	Symbol
Ali	Turkey	lira	TL

Discuss these questions with your classmates.

1. Do you like the idea of using other things, such as tea or stones, in place of money?

2. Is money the most important thing in life for you?

3. In the United States, people say, "Time is Money." Do you agree with this?

4. More and more people are using credit cards. Do you think that one day coins and paper bills will go out of use?

comparing with *as . . . as*

When we compare two things that are the same, we use **as** + **adjective** + **as.**

Example:

> Big stones can be **as big as** two tall men.
>
> Small stones are **as big as** dinner plates.

For the negative form, we use **not as** + **adjective** + **as**.

Example:

> A dime is **not as big as** a quarter.
>
> Salt is **not as expensive as** tea.

Exercise 1

Make sentences with the words below. Use the verb **be.**
When you see the = symbol, use **as . . . as.**
When you see the < symbol, use **not as . . . as.**

1. a small stone = a dinner plate   (big)

   A small stone is as big as a dinner plate.

2. paper bills < coins   (heavy)

   _____

   _____

3. a cent = a dime   (small)

   _____

   _____

4. apples = oranges   (expensive)

   _____

   _____

5. time = money in the United States   (important)

   _____

   _____

6. tea = money in some countries   (valuable)

_____

_____

Work alone, with a partner, or in a group.
Review of comparative: Use as . . . as, -er . . . than, or more . . . than

1. A paper bill in my country/United States dollar bill. (big)

_____

_____

2. A car in the United States/a car in my country. (expensive)

_____

_____

3. Money/time in my country. (important)

_____

_____

1. Write sentences.

Answer these questions with complete sentences.

a. What is the name of the currency (money) in your country?

_____

_____

b. Are the paper bills in your country all one color or different colors? What colors are they?

_____

_____

c. Are the paper bills in your country as big as the U.S. dollar bill or bigger?

_____

_____

d. What is the smallest paper bill? What can you buy with it?

_____

_____

e. Are people in your country today using credit cards?

_____

_____

f. Do you think that one day everybody in your country will use credit cards in place of money?

_____

_____

2. Rewrite in paragraph form.

Rewrite your sentences in the form of a paragraph.

Checklist

_____ Did you indent the first line?

_____ Did you give a title to your sentences?

_____ Did you write the title with a capital letter?

_____ Did you put the title in the center of the top of the page?

_____ Did you write on every other line?

3. Edit your work.

Work with a partner or your teacher to edit your sentences. Correct spelling, punctuation, vocabulary, and grammar.

4. Write your final copy.

Chapter 12: Perfume

··

Discuss these questions with your classmates or teacher.

1 What is your favorite perfume?

2 Why do people use perfume?

3 What is perfume made from?

Reading: Perfume

A long time ago people found a way to create a nice smell. They put nice-smelling wood or leaves into a fire. A nice smell came **through** the smoke. That is how we got the word "perfume." In Latin "per" means "through," and "fumus" means "smoke."

Perfume is not so simple today. A perfume **expert** can tell the difference between nineteen thousand different smells. Some of these smells are from **chemicals**; they are not from real flowers. For a very good perfume today, the expert mixes more than one hundred **ingredients**.

Today, perfume has other uses too. Plastic that smells like **leather** is just one example. Also, scientists are finding that some smells make us feel better. They help us to relax, to sleep, or to feel happier. Scientists found that the smell of apples with **spices** can make our **blood pressure** go down. In the future we may use perfume in a **completely** different way.

Complete the definitions with the words or phrases below.

an expert   through   chemicals
an ingredient   leather   spices
blood pressure   completely

1. Another word for "totally" is

   _____.

2. A person who is very good at his job is

   _____.

3. Things that are made by chemistry are called

   _____.

4. One of a mixture of things from which something is made is

   _____.

5. Animal skin from which things like shoes and bags are made is

   called _____.

6. Salt, pepper, and dried plants that give taste to foods are called

   _____.

7. When something goes from one end to the other, it comes

   _____.

8. To measure how your blood travels through your body, a doctor or

   nurse may take your _____.

A. Looking for the Main Ideas

Write complete answers to these questions.

1. What does the word "perfume" mean in Latin?

   _____

   _____

2. How many ingredients does an expert mix for a very good perfume today?

   _____

   _____

3. How can some smells help you?

   _____

   _____

B. Looking for Details

One word in each sentence is not correct. Rewrite the sentence with the correct word.

1. A long time ago people put nice-smelling plastic or leaves into a fire.

   _____

   _____

2. A perfume expert can tell the difference between ninety thousand different smells.

   _____

   _____

3. Some of the ingredients in perfume today are not from real people.

_____

_____

4. Smoke that smells like leather is an example.

_____

_____

5. The smell of apples with spices can make our blood pressure go through.

_____

_____

DISCUSSION

Discuss these questions with your classmates.

1. Some people do not like the smell of other people's perfume in the air around them. Do you think the use of perfume should be stopped?
2. Some smells make us feel better. What smells make you feel better?
3. How do think perfume can be used in the future?

too or *very* + Adjective

Very goes before an adjective. It emphasizes an adjective. It has a positive meaning.

Example:

> For a **very** good perfume, the expert uses more than one hundred ingredients.

> You must not confuse **very** with **too**. **Too** goes before an adjective. It gives the idea of "more than necessary." **Too** gives a negative meaning.

Examples:

> That smell is **too** sweet. (I don't like it)
> That smell is **very** sweet. (I like it.)

Exercise 1

Complete the sentences with **too or very.**

1. This smell is _____ good. I like it.

2. I don't like this smell. It's _____ strong for me.

3. She likes a strong perfume. This is _____ soft for her.

4. The smell of fresh bread makes me _____ hungry.

5. This perfume is _____ expensive. I can never buy it.

6. I love the smell of this rose. It's _____ delicate.

Two Meanings of *too*

Too changes its meaning with the position it has in a sentence.

Examples:

> This perfume is **too** strong. (I don't like it)
> I like that perfume and this one **too**. (also)

We use **too** at the end of an affirmative sentence to mean "also."

Rewrite the sentences using **too** *in the correct place.*

1. I don't like this smell. (strong)

   _____

2. That perfume has a strong smell, and it is also expensive.

   _____

3. The perfume has real flowers, and it also has some chemicals.

   _____

4. I didn't buy that perfume. (expensive)

   _____

5. The smell of the sea makes me feel relaxed and also happy.

   _____

6. Please don't use that perfume. (heavy)

   _____

WRITING PRACTICE

1. Write sentences.

Answer these questions with complete sentences.

a. What is your favorite perfume or smell?

_____

_____

b. How often do you use it or smell it?

_____

_____

c. Why do you use perfume?

_____

_____

d. Are there are any other perfumes or smells that you like?

_____

_____

e. Are there any smells or perfumes that you don't like?

_____

_____

f. Do you think it is important to have nice smells? Why or why not?

_____

_____

g. Do you think people have the right to use perfume when other people may not like it?

_____

_____

2. Rewrite in paragraph form.

Rewrite your sentences in the form of a paragraph.

Checklist

_____ Did you indent the first line?

_____ Did you give a title to your sentences?

_____ Did you write the title with a capital letter?

_____ Did you put the title in the center of the top of the page?

_____ Did you write on every other line?

3. Edit your work.

Work with a partner or your teacher to edit your sentences. Correct spelling, punctuation, vocabulary, and grammar.

4. Write your final copy.

INVENTIONS QUIZ

Test your knowledge. Circle the correct answer.

1. How many countries use a dollar?
   a. 10
   b. 22
   c. 47

2. How long have we had bicycles?
   a. 500 years
   b. 150 years
   c. 50 years

3. Who discovered paper?
   a. The Chinese
   b. The Arabs
   c. The Aztecs

4. When did people first use aspirin tablets?
   a. In 1820
   b. In 1949
   c. In 1915

5. Different countries use different money. Match the money with the country.

   1. mark   _____   a. Greece
   2. drachma   _____   b. China
   3. yuan   _____   c. Brazil
   4. riyal   _____   d. Germany
   5. cruzeiro _____   e. Saudi Arabia

UNIT 7

People

Chapter 13: Wilma Rudolf

PRE-READING QUESTIONS

Discuss these questions with your classmates or teacher.

1 Describe the woman in the photo.

2 Why do you think the woman is holding the medals?

Reading: Wilma Rudolf

Wilma Rudolf was born in Clarksville, Tennessee, in 1940. There were twenty-two children in her family. Wilma was not a strong child. When she was very young, she got a disease called **polio**. Wilma's leg began to have problems. Wilma's family loved and helped her. Her mother and her sisters **massaged** her bad leg. The doctor put a **brace** on her leg for six years. One lucky day when she was twelve, the doctor took off the brace.

At high school Wilma started to run. Soon she won every **race** she ran. At age fifteen she prepared for the **national** races. She won all nine of the races. The next year, 1956, Wilma was in the Olympic games in Australia. Wilma came back with a **bronze medal**.

In 1960 Wilma went to the Olympic games in Italy. The weather was very hot just as it was in Tennessee. The Italians **cheered** her. Wilma **won** the 100 meter, 200 meter, and the 400 meter relay. Wilma Rudolf was the first American woman to win three Olympic gold medals.

In 1963 Wilma got her **degree** in education. That year she married her high school sweetheart, and now they have four children.

Complete the definitions with the words below.

massage	brace	bronze medal
Polio	race	win
degree	cheer	national

1. _____ is a serious disease that can even make a person disabled.

2. To rub or press your hands on a body to increase the flow of blood is to _____.

3. When you run to see who is the fastest, it is a _____.

4. A person who runs to be the first in his country, runs in a _____ race.

5. When you come in first in a race, you _____.

6. In the Olympics, you can win a gold medal, a silver medal, or a _____.

7. When you support a person to win, you _____ him/her.

8. Something that you can use to support part of your body is a _____.

9. When you go to a university and graduate, you get a _____.

A. Looking for the Main Ideas

Circle the letter of the correct answer.

1. When she was young, Wilma had problems with her

   _____.

   a. doctor

   b. mother

   c. leg

2. At high school Wilma _____.

   a. started to run and won every race

   b. started to run with a brace

   c. ran for Australia

3. In the Olympic games of 1960, Wilma

   _____.

   a. won a bronze medal

   b. won three gold medals

   c. won because she was a woman

B. Looking for Details

Circle T if the sentence is true. Circle F if the sentence is false.

1. Wilma was a strong child.	T	F
2. Wilma had a brace on her leg for twelve years.	T	F
3. When she was fifteen, she ran for the national races.	T	F
4. In 1956 the Olympic games were in Italy.	T	F
5. Wilma won three gold medals in 1960.	T	F
6. Wilma got married in 1963.	T	F

DISCUSSION

Discuss these qustions with your classmates.

1. What sports people do you know with health or physical problems? How have they overcome their problems?

2. Do you think that if you work hard and believe in something, you will get it? Give an example of someone who did just that.

3. Think of someone famous. Do not say his/her name. Tell your partner or the class about this person's life. Can they guess who it is?

WRITING SKILLS

Telling About Someone's Life

Read the following facts about Wilma Rudolf's life.

> The Story of Wilma Rudolf

1940	– Wilma is born in Clarksville, Tennessee. She is not a strong child. In the next few years she gets polio. Her leg begins to have problems.
1946	– The doctor puts a brace on her leg.
1952	– The doctor takes off the brace.
1955	– In high school Wilma wins every race she runs. She prepares for the national races.
1956	– Wilma is in the Olympic Games in Australia. She comes back with a bronze medal.
1960	– Wilma goes to the Olympic Games in Italy. She is the first American woman to win three Olympic gold medals.
1963	– Wilma gets her degree in education. She marries her childhood sweetheart.

Write the story of Wilma Rudolf in the past tense.

1940   *Wilma was born in Clarksville, Tennessee. She was*
          not a strong child. In the next few years
          she got polio

1946   –_____

1952   –_____

1955   –_____

1956   –_____

1960   –_____

1963   –_____

Exercise 2

Now write the story of your life. Use the present or the past tense.

The following models will help you:

> I go(went) to high school/elementary school/college.
> I graduate (graduated) from high school/college.

The Story of _____

19___ *I was born in* _____

_____

_____

_____

19___ _____

_____

_____

19___ _____

_____

_____

19___ _____

_____

_____

19___ _____

_____

19___ _____

_____

_____

Different Ways of Saying *when*

Read the following paragraph about Wilma Rudolf.

In 1940 Wilma is born in Clarksville, Tennessee. She is not a strong child. In the next few years she gets polio. Her leg begins to have problems. In 1946 the doctor puts a brace on her leg. In 1952 the doctor takes off the brace. In 1955 Wilma wins every race she runs in high school. In 1956 Wilma is in the Olympic games in Australia. She comes back with a bronze medal.

In the paragraph above there are too many sentences that begin in the same way:

> In 1940 . . .
> In 1946 . . .
> In 1952 . . .
> In 1956 . . .

Underline these in the paragraph above.
We can change some of these in this way:

In 1946 . . .
{ At age six,
  When she is six,

In 1952 . . .
{ At age twelve,
  When she is twelve,
  Six years later

In 1955 . . .
{ At age fifteen,
  When she is fifteen,
  Three years later

In 1956 . . .
{ The next year
  At age sixteen,
  One year later

Look at the same paragraph about Wilma Rudolf. Use a different beginning in each of the blank spaces.

In 1940 Wilma is born in Clarksville, Tennessee. She is not a strong

child. In the next few years she gets polio. Her leg begins to have

problems. _____ the doctor puts

a brace on her leg. _____ the

doctor takes off the brace. _____

Wilma wins every race she runs in high school.

_____ Wilma is in the Olympic

games in Australia. She comes back with a bronze medal.

2. Rewrite in paragraph form.

Step 1: *Rewrite the sentences about your life (see page 19) in the form of a paragraph.*

Step 2: *Rewrite your paragraph again with only one "In 19____" at the beginning of a sentence. Use other words with the same meaning.*

Checklist

_____ Did you indent the first line?

_____ Did you give a title to your sentence?

_____ Did you write the title with a capital letter?

_____ Did you put the title in the center of the top of the page?

_____ Did you write on every other line?

3. Edit your work.

Work with a partner or your teacher to edit your sentences. Correct spelling, punctuation, vocabulary, and grammar.

4. Write your final copy.

Chapter 14: An Wang

Discuss these questions with your classmates or teacher.

1 Describe thc man in the picture.

2 Why do you think he is famous?

Reading: An Wang

An Wang was born in Shanghai, China, in 1920. He came to America as an **immigrant** at age twenty-five. He studied at Harvard, a famous university near Boston. He was very intelligent and soon got a **doctorate** from Harvard.

In 1951 An Wang started a small company. The company was Wang Laboratories. It had only one room and two **employees**. The company made **calculators** and **computers**. Each year the company grew and grew. By 1985 Wang had thirty thousand employees and had made $3 billion. Wang was one of the most **successful** computer companies in the world.

Money did not change An Wang. He lived with his wife in the same house outside Boston. He had only two **suits** at one time, and they were always gray. An Wang's life was his company. He made his son, Fred, president of the company in 1986. The company began to have problems.

Wang died in 1990. People in America will remember this great man. He was **generous** and liked to give money. We find his name in places like the Wang Center for the Performing Arts or the Wang Institute in Boston.

VOCABULARY

Rewrite each sentence, replacing the underlined words with one of the words or phrases below.

employees	an immigrant	a doctorate
calculators	computers	suits
most successful	generous	

1. An Wang came from China as <u>a person coming into a country to live there</u>.

   _____

   _____

2. He studied at Harvard and got <u>the highest degree given by a university</u>.

   _____

   _____

3. In 1951 Wang Laboratories had only two <u>people who were paid workers</u> .

   _____

   _____

4. Wang Laboratories made <u>small machines that can do all kinds of work with numbers</u>.

   _____

   _____

5. Wang Laboratories also made <u>machines that store and recall information and find answers very quickly</u>.

   _____

   _____

6. Wang was one of the world's <u>best</u> computer companies.

_____

_____

7. An Wang always wore gray <u>sets of clothes made of the same</u> <u>material</u>.

_____

_____

8. An Wang was <u>ready to give money and help</u>.

_____

_____

A. Looking for the Main Ideas

Circle the letter of the correct answer.

1. An Wang came from _____.

    a. China

    b. Harvard

    c. Boston

2. In 1951 Wang Laboratories _____.

    a. was the most successful company in the world

    b. was a small company

    c. had 30,000 employees

3. Wang's life was his _____.

    a. money

    b. house

    c. company

B. Looking for Details

One word in each sentence is not correct. Rewrite the sentence with the correct word.

1. An Wang was born in 1925.

    _____

    _____

2. He got a doctorate from Boston.

    _____

    _____

3. In 1951 Wang Laboratories had only two rooms.

    _____

    _____

4. Wang made laboratories and computers.

_____

_____

5. By 1985 Wang had thirty thousand companies.

_____

_____

6. An Wang had only two computers at one time.

_____

_____

DISCUSSION

Discuss these questions with your classmates.

1. Do you know of another immigrant who came to America with very little and then became very successful? Tell us about that person.

2. Some people want to be very rich or very famous. Other people just want to have an ordinary life. What do you want? Give reasons.

3. An Wang was one of the richest men in the world but liked to live in the same house. Money did not change him. Imagine that you just became a millionaire. Will your life change very much? Describe your new life.

WRITING SKILLS

Asking Questions

Asking the right questions is important when you write. In the exercise below, you will write questions for the sentences.

Exercise 1

Write the questions for these answers.

1. _____?

   I was born in Tokyo, Japan.

2. _____?

   I was born in 1977.

3. _____?

   My father is an engineer.

4. _____?

   My mother is a housewife.

5. _____?

   I have two brothers and one sister.

6. _____?

   I went to high school in Tokyo.

7. _____?

   I graduated from high school in 1993.

8. _____?

   Right now I am studying English.

9. _____?

   In the future, I want to go to an American university.

10. _____?

    I want to study design.

Prepositions of Time

In

We use **in** with years or months.

Examples:

> **In** 1985 . . .
>
> **In** January . . .

From . . . to . . .

We use **from** for the beginning of the action and **to** for the end of the action.

Examples:

> I went to high school **from** 1989 **from** 1989 **to** 1993.
>
> I work **from** nine **to** five.
>
> She was on vacation **from** July 15 **to** August 15.

For

We use **for** to show how long.

Examples:

> I studied English **for** three years.
>
> I stayed in New York **for** ten days.

Exercise 2

Write the prepositions in the blanks.

1. I arrived in Boston _____ August for the summer.

2. He lived in Tokyo _____ sixteen years.

3. She worked for that company _____ 1989

   _____ 1993.

4. He graduated from high school _____ 1990.

5. He worked for the company _____ fifteen years.

6. He worked _____ six in the morning

   _____ eight at night.

7. An Wang died _____ 1990.

8. I am going back _____ December for my vacation.

WRITING PRACTICE

1. Write questions and answers.

Work with a partner. Find out about your partner's life. Ask questions about the past, present, and future.

These prompts may help you:

> *Where/when born?*
> *How many brothers and sisters/have?*
> *When/go/high school? Where/go/high school?*
> *What/study/now?*
> *Where/study/now?*
> *What/do/in the future?*
> *Why?*

> *Include any other questions you like.*

Write the answers to the questions.

2. Rewrite in paragraph form.

Rewrite your sentences in the form of a paragraph. Use your partner's name as the title.

Checklist

_____ Did you indent the first line?

_____ Did you give a title to your sentences?

_____ Did you write the title with a capital letter?

_____ Did you put the title in the center of the top of the page?

_____ Did you write on every other line?

3. Edit your work.

Work with a partner or your teacher to edit your sentences. Correct spelling, punctuation, vocabulary, and grammar.

4. Write your final copy.

WHO . . .

1. . . . **said**

> *And so, my fellow Americans, ask not what your country can do for you; ask what you can do for your country.*

. . . **was** president of the United States.

. . . **died in** 1963.

---

2. . . . **said**

> *I remain just one thing, and one thing only—and that is a clown.*

. . . **was** a comedian.

. . . **made** silent movies.

. . . **was famous** for his hat and cane.

---

3. . . . **said**

> *If you want anything said, ask a man. If you want anything done, ask a woman.*

. . . **was born** in England.

. . . **studied** at Oxford University.

. . . **became** prime minister in 1979.
